GW00600663

THE
WONDERS OF
NATURE

ISBN: 0 946994 10 2

This edition created and produced
by Christensen Press Ltd for:

Ebury Press
National Magazine House
72 Broadwick Street
London W1V 2BP

First published in 1985 in Australia by:

Golden Press Pty Ltd
incorporated in NSW
P.O. Box 390
Drummoyne 2047
Australia

and in New Zealand by:

Golden Press
717 Rosebank Road
Rosebank
Avondale, Auckland
New Zealand

Printed and bound by Grafica Editoriale, Italy.
Typesetting by Pre-Print Photosetting (Leeds) Limited.
Colour separation by RCS Graphics Ltd and
Paramount Litho Ltd.

THE
WONDERS OF
NATURE

by Elisabeth Sackett

Designed by David Nash

Contents

The World We Do Not See

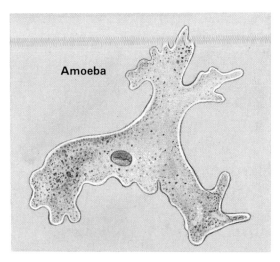

Amoeba

The simplest and smallest animals on this planet are called protozoans. These creatures are single-celled and most are far too small to be seen with the unaided eye. Protozoans are extremely varied. Some are naked blobs of jelly. Others are covered in hundreds of tiny hairs called cilia, or have one or two hair-like whips called flagella.

Protozoans need food and water to survive. Many live in fresh or salt water, but large numbers live inside, or on the outside, of other animals. Some of these cause disease and are known as parasites. For example, sleeping sickness and malaria are both caused by parasites.

The simplest forms of animal life are protozoans. They are single-celled animals and there are a great many different varieties. Some, like the amoeba above, are blobs of jelly. Others, like chlamydomonas, have long whip-like hairs, called flagella.

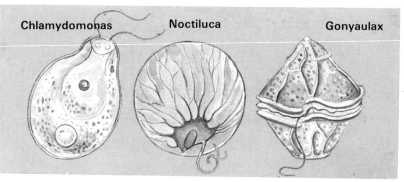

Chlamydomonas   Noctiluca   Gonyaulax

Below: The protozoan, didinium, uses its flagellum to catch food. Here it is shown piercing another protozoan, paramecium, with it. It then gradually sucks the paramecium in and digests it. A paramecium is covered with tiny hairs called cilia, which it uses for moving and feeding.

Each kind of protozoan has its own distinctive way of moving and eating. Some move along by waving their cilia. The cilia are also used to draw food into the gullet. Other protozoans use their whip-like flagellum to propel themselves along. The flagellum is also used to catch food. The amoeba pushes out fingers of jelly when it needs to move, and feeds by flowing around its prey and engulfing it.

Didinium pierces a paramecium

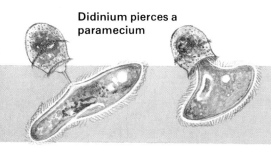

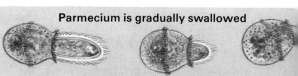

Parmecium is gradually swallowed

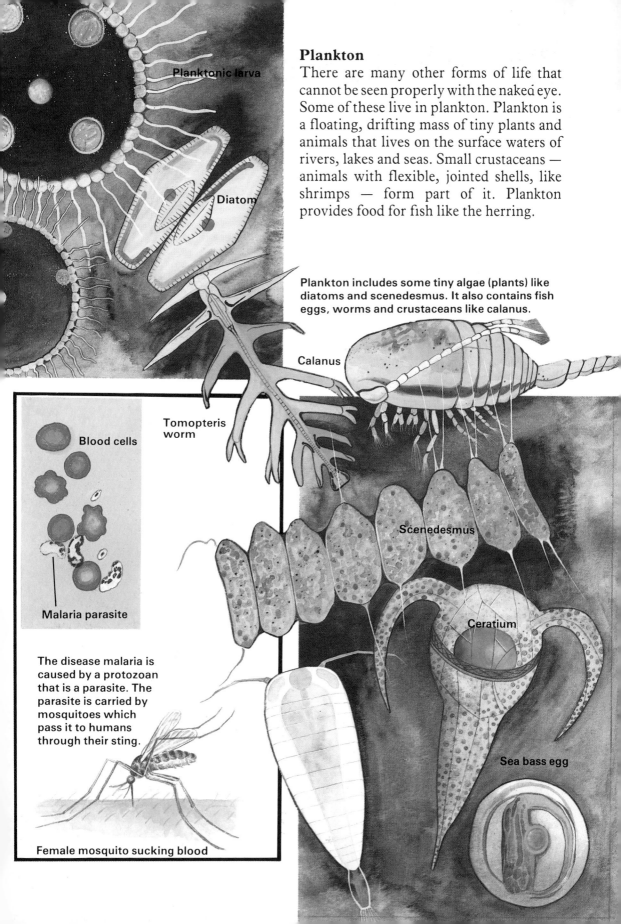

Planktonic larva

Diatom

Plankton

There are many other forms of life that cannot be seen properly with the naked eye. Some of these live in plankton. Plankton is a floating, drifting mass of tiny plants and animals that lives on the surface waters of rivers, lakes and seas. Small crustaceans — animals with flexible, jointed shells, like shrimps — form part of it. Plankton provides food for fish like the herring.

Plankton includes some tiny algae (plants) like diatoms and scenedesmus. It also contains fish eggs, worms and crustaceans like calanus.

Calanus

Tomopteris worm

Blood cells

Malaria parasite

The disease malaria is caused by a protozoan that is a parasite. The parasite is carried by mosquitoes which pass it to humans through their sting.

Female mosquito sucking blood

Scenedesmus

Ceratium

Sea bass egg

Feeding Time

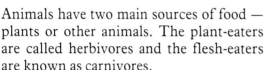

Animals have two main sources of food — plants or other animals. The plant-eaters are called herbivores and the flesh-eaters are known as carnivores.

Carnivores hunt in different ways. Cheetahs and other members of the cat family stalk their prey; then with a sudden spring, or after a swift chase, they kill their victim. Wolves and wild dogs hunt in packs. By running together they can kill animals larger than themselves. The red fox prefers to hunt alone. It also eats plants and berries. Animals that eat plants as well as flesh are called omnivores.

Above: Whales have large comb-like plates in their mouths through which they strain small crustaceans called krill.

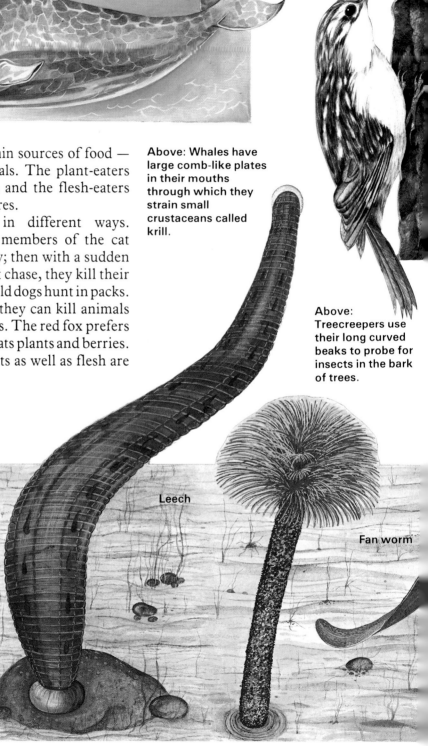

Above: Treecreepers use their long curved beaks to probe for insects in the bark of trees.

Right: Leeches have a sucker at each end of their body. Some species feed on the blood of other animals. They attach themselves by the hind sucker and pierce their prey with three teeth inside the head sucker. They then suck the victim's blood. Fan worms collet tiny food particles with their tentacles.

Leech

Fan worm

The leopard has to run very swiftly to catch the gazelles which live on the great plains of Africa.

Cuttlefish have ten tentacles; two are larger than the others. It catches prey such as prawns with the suckers on its long tentacles.

Cuttlefish

Flatwarm

ding
be

Many flatworms feed on debris at the bottom of ponds. They have a tube with a mouth at the end. This acts like a vacuum cleaner, sucking in particles of food.

Each animal is specially adapted to its way of feeding. Birds of prey, for example, have very keen eyesight for spotting animals such as mice on the ground. They also have strong talons and a sharp beak for seizing their prey and tearing it apart.

Herbivores are generally peaceful animals and different species often feed together. Giraffes and gazelles will eat, at different heights, from the same acacia tree. Many herbivores, such as elephants, have to travel great distances in order to find enough food.

11

How Animals Move

All animals are capable of some kind of movement. While some, such as the cheetah, move with amazing speed, others like the sloth, seem reluctant to move at all. Animals need to move to find food or escape enemies, or to find others of their own kind.

Members of the cat family are among some of the swiftest animals on land. The cheetah can run at up to 105 kilometres an hour. But many animals can only move very slowly. Often they are herbivores that do not need speed to catch prey. These animals cannot escape from enemies by running away and have other ways of defending themselves. Turtles and snails, for example, have shells to retreat into. Creatures such as caterpillars are usually the same colour as the leaves they feed on, and so are hard to find. Other slow-moving animals, especially some of the insects, produce chemicals that put off predators. Many animals protect themselves by staying hidden during the day, only coming out to feed at night.

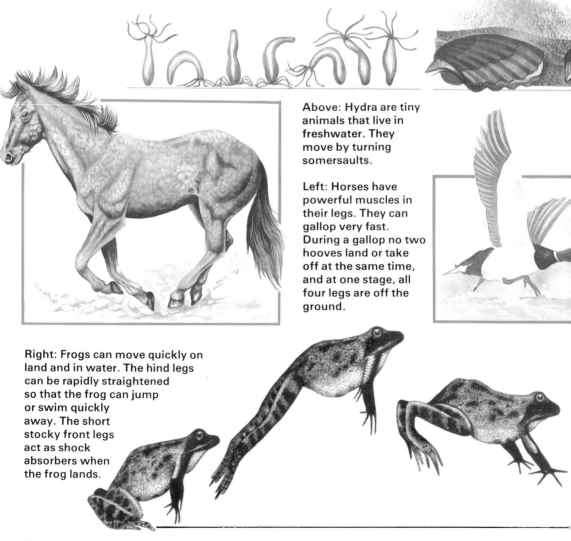

Above: Hydra are tiny animals that live in freshwater. They move by turning somersaults.

Left: Horses have powerful muscles in their legs. They can gallop very fast. During a gallop no two hooves land or take off at the same time, and at one stage, all four legs are off the ground.

Right: Frogs can move quickly on land and in water. The hind legs can be rapidly straightened so that the frog can jump or swim quickly away. The short stocky front legs act as shock absorbers when the frog lands.

Animals without legs

Animals without legs have their own special ways of moving. Hydra, for example, turn somersaults and scallops propel themselves along by opening and closing their shells. Earthworms anchor a part of their body with tiny bristles, called chaetae, while the rest of the body moves forward. Sea urchins move by tiny tubes called tube feet which extend from their bodies. Suction-like discs at the end of the tubes hold firmly to the rock surface over which the sea urchin is moving. Fish swim by moving their bodies from side to side and steer with their tail and fins.

Flight

Most birds and many insects move mainly by flying. Birds have light bodies and wings covered with feathers. The spine-tailed swift can fly at up to 170 kilometres an hour, faster than any other animal can move. Some seabirds and birds of prey can stay in the air for long periods of time by soaring on air currents.

Bats are the only mammals capable of flight. Instead of wings covered with feathers, they have folds of skin. Other mammals, such as flying squirrels, which appear to be flying from tree to tree are really only gliding.

Above: Scallops swim through the water using a form of jet propulsion. As they open and close their shells water is taken in and shot out again.

Water birds do not find take-off very easy. Some flap their wings and rise directly from the water, but others, such as the mallard (left), have to flap their wings and run along the water's surface to get airborne.

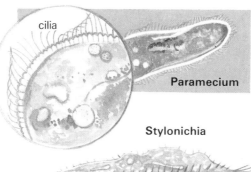

cilia

Paramecium

Stylonichia

Left: The protozoan paramecium rows itself through the water by waving its tiny hairs called cilia. The enlargement shows the movement of the cilia.

Another protozoan, stylonichia, uses its cilia to crawl along.

Animal Buildings

Animals like the moose and the elephant which spend their lives moving in search of food do not make permanent homes. The female gives birth to her young and brings them up in the open. These animals often move in large groups which help to protect the young animals. But many animals build places where they live or raise their young. Other creatures build special structures to help them catch prey.

Some animals, such as the badger, rabbit and beaver, build homes that they live in year after year. Sometimes these homes are complicated structures. Sometimes they are small and simply built. They all provide shelter and safety for the animals and their young.

Tailorbird

Badgers live in 'sets' deep beneath the ground. Sets have many entrances, tunnels and chambers. The nesting chamber, where the young are born, is lined with moss and dried grass.

Many animals, especially birds, build in trees. The squirrel makes a comfortable nest of leaves amongst branches. Animal homes are also found underground and the tunnels may extend for long distances. Prairie dogs live in burrows which may stretch over many acres.

Many kinds of worms live in tubes. The mason worm, for example, cements a tube around itself made from sand, mud and shell fragments.

Top: Tailorbirds sew two leaves together with plant fibres to make their nests.

Right: Weaver birds weave an elaborate nest from grass and twigs. The nest hangs from a branch.

Weaver bird

Spinners

Most spider webs are made to catch prey. The water spider however, actually spins a home for itself underwater. It can breathe there because it fills the bell-shaped dome with air bubbles that it carries from the surface.

Other spiders, like the garden spider, spin a beautiful orb-shaped web between the branches of plants. The spider hides at the edge of the web waiting for insects to be caught on the sticky silk threads. The garden spider also spins to protect her eggs. She makes a cocoon around them and disguises it with bits of bark and dust.

Insect Builders

Many termites build nests above the ground. These nests are usually very large and some have 'chimneys'. These keep the termite mound cool: warm air rises through passages in the walls, loses its heat and flows back downwards. Inside the mound is a maze of tunnels and chambers.

Some insects build special structures to raise their young in. The potter wasp, for example, makes small pots of clay which it attaches to plants. It places a caterpillar inside the pot and lays an egg there. When the wasp larva hatches it feeds on the caterpillar.

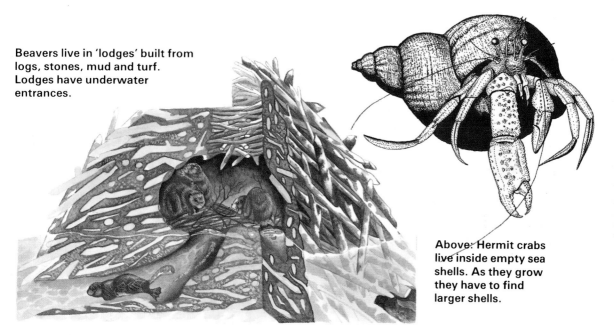

Beavers live in 'lodges' built from logs, stones, mud and turf. Lodges have underwater entrances.

Above: Hermit crabs live inside empty sea shells. As they grow they have to find larger shells.

Above: Wood ants live in large colonies. They build nests with many tunnels and chambers.

The Master Builder

The beaver is, perhaps, the greatest engineer of them all. It likes to build its 'lodge' of branches and twigs in the middle of shallow, slow-moving waters. And where conditions are not ideal, it will build a dam across the stream to transform the upstream side into a calm lake in which to build its home. The lodge, with its living chamber and passages, may rise over two metres above the surface of the water.

15

Breeding Habits

Many animals such as the badger, live and breed in the same place. Others often travel great distances to have their young. Caribou move from the forests of North America to the Arctic tundra to breed. Birds, like the house martin, that have migrated south for the winter, return thousands of kilometres north to lay their eggs.

Below: Salmon migrate from the oceans to freshwater streams when they breed. They swim against strong currents and often leap up waterfalls as they move upstream to lay their eggs.

Finding a mate

Most animals have special ways to attract a mate. Male frogs and toads make their way back to water and croak loudly; grasshoppers chirp and birds sing. Mammals and insects, in particular, produce special scents. Male mammals often mark their territories during the breeding season to keep other males away. Competition for a female may be very fierce, and sometimes leads to fighting. Birds and fish often have elaborate courtship displays. Once a male has attracted a female's attention he may put on a display to persuade her to mate with him.

Nest Building

Birds whose young are well developed when they hatch often do not build nests. Sandpipers and plovers lay their eggs in shallow depressions on the ground. The fairy tern glues its eggs to a branch. An emperor penguin holds its eggs on its feet until the young are hatched.

Many birds though construct secure nests. Nests are made from a variety of materials, such as twigs, grass, feathers, mud and sheep's wool. Some birds have simple cup-shaped nests, like the robin, which makes a nest of twigs and stalks, lined with mud and grass. Other birds make more

Above: The male midwife toad carries strings of eggs wrapped around his hind feet until they hatch.

Woodpecker eggs

Above: The woodpecker excavates a nest in a dead tree. Its eggs hatch after ten days.

Left: The mallee fowl lays its eggs in a pit which it digs and fills with plants.

Left: Sea turtles come ashore at night to lay their eggs. They crawl up the beach and dig a hole where they lay hundreds of them. When they hatch, the tiny baby turtles have a long, dangerous journey back to the sea.

elaborate nests which are completely enclosed except for a small opening.

Once the eggs have been laid they must be incubated. In many species of bird both parents share this job, one sitting on the eggs while the other provides food. But the mallee fowl of Australia buries its eggs and leaves the chicks to hatch by themselves.

Animals and their Young

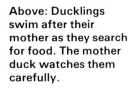

Above: Ducklings swim after their mother as they search for food. The mother duck watches them carefully.

Right: A female cuckoo does not look after her young. She lays her egg in another bird's nest. This nest belongs to a meadow pipit. The cuckoo hatches and pushes out the meadow pipit's eggs. The meadow pipit feeds the young cuckoo until it flies away from the nest.

A human baby would not be able to survive without the care and attention of its parents. Not all animals take such care of their young. Most fishes and insects, once they have laid their eggs, have nothing more to do with their offspring.

Most animals that take little or no care of their young produce great numbers of them. A cod can lay up to eight million eggs at one time but only a few will survive to be adults. There are some fishes, such as the seahorse and tilapia, who look after their young, but they lay far fewer eggs.

Caring Parents

Animals that take great care of their young have only a few at one time. Monkeys and apes usually give birth to only one baby at a time and care for it with great devotion for many months. Hunting animals, like the large cats and some wild dogs, have to provide food for their young even after they are weaned from their mother's milk. These youngsters have to gradually learn how to hunt for their own food. Meanwhile, they are also groomed and protected until they can care for themselves.

Most birds make very good parents. Once the eggs have been laid the mother sits on them until they are hatched. After the chicks have hatched the parents have to work very hard to feed them. Usually both parents share this duty, but in some cases, such as the mallard duck, the female cares for the eggs and ducklings alone.

Baby Sitting

Some animal mothers do not have to care for their young alone. They have help from other members of the family. The mother wolf can go hunting and leave her cubs safely with an 'aunt'. The mother elephant has another female to help her look after her calf until it can care for itself.

Sticklebacks with their nest

Tilapia

Rhinoceros

Fox with cubs

Top: The male stickleback builds a nest for the female to lay her eggs in. The male stands guard over the nest until the eggs hatch.

Above: When danger threatens, the tilapia takes its young into its mouth until the danger has passed.

Above: Large mammals, like the rhino, usually have only one baby. Smaller ones like the fox have several. Young mammals thrive on their mother's rich milk.

Right: A newly born kangaroo is very small. It climbs into its mother's pouch and lives there for six months. Then it gradually spends more and more time out of the pouch.

19

Life Stories

Some animals are born, or hatch from eggs, looking very similar to the adult animal. They learn to move and feed very quickly and are able to run or hide if danger threatens. The wildebeest of Africa has young that are able to run with the herd within a day of birth. Young crocodiles are miniature versions of the adult and feed and swim soon after they hatch from the egg.

Many other animals start life naked, blind and quite helpless. They are protected and fed by their parents until they become strong enough to look after themselves. They must learn to feed, keep

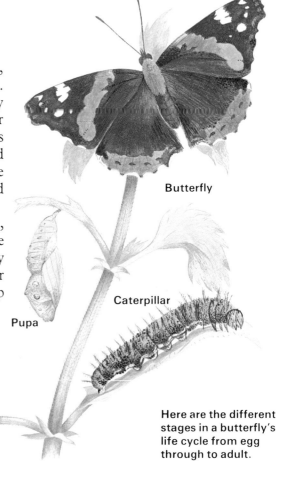

Butterfly

Pupa

Caterpillar

Eggs

Here are the different stages in a butterfly's life cycle from egg through to adult.

Bee visiting a flower to feed on nectar

FLOWERING PLANTS

Flowering plants produce seeds that can eventually grow into new plants. Seeds are formed when the plant is pollinated. Pollen is often carried from flower to flower by insects which feed on the flowers' nectar. The pollen fertilizes the female parts of the flower, called ovules, and seeds form.

The ripe seeds may be blown away, or eaten by animals and passed out through their droppings. If a seed lands in a suitable place, it will start to grow. The seed cracks and a root pushes down into the soil. A shoot grows upwards and the first leaves soon unfold.

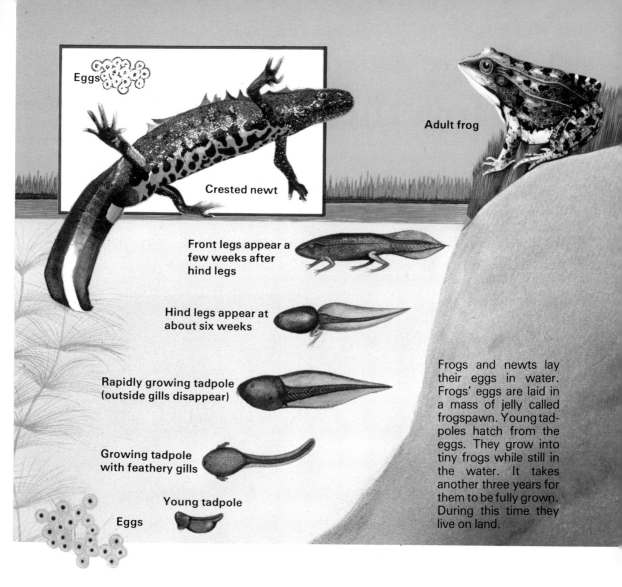

Eggs

Crested newt

Adult frog

Front legs appear a few weeks after hind legs

Hind legs appear at about six weeks

Rapidly growing tadpole (outside gills disappear)

Growing tadpole with feathery gills

Young tadpole

Eggs

Frogs and newts lay their eggs in water. Frogs' eggs are laid in a mass of jelly called frogspawn. Young tadpoles hatch from the eggs. They grow into tiny frogs while still in the water. It takes another three years for them to be fully grown. During this time they live on land.

clean and defend themselves. Young birds and rodents need only a few weeks of care but other animals take many months or, like the elephant, several years to become independent.

Metamorphosis

Insects and amphibians — animals such as frogs and newts — start life as eggs and go through several changes before becoming adults. This type of development is called metamorphosis which means 'to change form'. The greenfly, however, is one insect that does not develop this way; instead it gives birth to live young.

The Wonderful Transformation

The life cycle of a butterfly has several amazing changes. The female butterfly lays her eggs on twigs, amongst flower buds or on the underside of leaves. The eggs hatch into caterpillars which eat vast quantities of the plant's leaves. As they grow larger, the caterpillars have to moult, or shed, their old skins. They moult several times.

When the caterpillar is fully grown it turns into a pupa. Inside the pupa, the caterpillar changes into a butterfly. The butterfly emerges from the pupa, dries its wings and flies away. It will soon be ready to look for a mate and start the life cycle all over again.

Living Together

Polar bears lead solitary lives in the frozen Arctic. They only come together with other polar bears in order to breed. Most kinds of bears, and several members of the cat family, such as the tiger and the leopard,

organized are those of baboons and mandrills. These troops can be as many as 300 strong, and have a strict social order.

One special kind of animal group is called a harem. During the breeding season one male animal gathers around him several females. Male fur seals form harems and fiercely battle with other males who try to take one of their wives.

A great many kinds of birds live together in flocks. Some, like the herring gull and starling, only live together in the autumn

Oxpecker

Oxpeckers ride on the backs of rhinos and eat the pests that live on their hides.

Right: Rattlesnakes are sometimes found in marmot burrows. Once, the two animals were thought to live in harmony. It is now believed the marmot provides the snake's next meal!

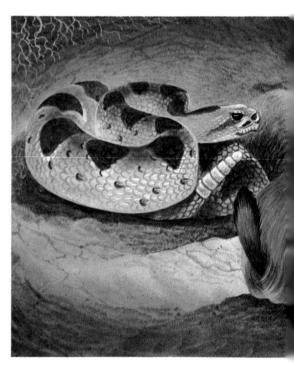

also spend most of their lives alone. Many other animals, however, live together in groups. Sometimes these groups are quite large.

Grazing animals such as deer, antelope, sheep and bison travel together in herds. Living in large numbers gives them protection from enemies. If a wolf pack attacks a herd of musk oxen, the males form a ring around the females and young calves.

Many species of monkey form communities known as troops. The most highly

and winter. But others, like the house sparrow and rook, spend their lives as part of a flock. Birds that live in large groups are expected to behave in a certain way and if they do not are expelled from the group.

Many bees and ants live in highly organized and disciplined communities. There are three main kinds of insect within these communities: a queen who lays eggs, male drones who mate with the queen, and workers. Each insect has its special duty within the nest.

Strange Partnerships

There are many useful partnerships between different animals. A crocodile will let an Egyptian plover pick out parasites from its skin and mouth. Ants keep aphids and 'milk' them but in return protect them from enemies. The hermit crab sometimes carries a sea anemone on its shell: the crab has camouflage and the anemone free transport to new feeding grounds. Some partnerships only benefit one partner. For example, many parasites which live in animals cause disease.

Goldfinches form pairs to breed but live in flocks at other times.

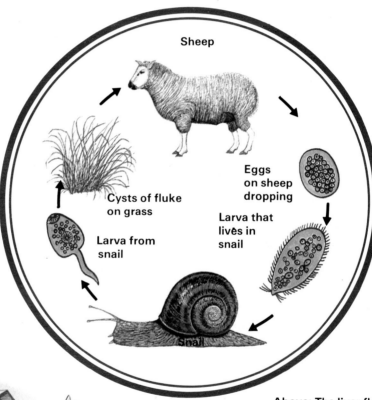

Sheep

Eggs on sheep dropping

Larva that lives in snail

Snail

Larva from snail

Cysts of fluke on grass

Above: The liver fluke lives in sheep and snails at different stages of its life cycle. It is a parasite.

Left: Bees live and work together in a hive or nest. Worker bees feed the young bee larvae in special comb cells.

23

Animal Senses and Communication

Left: The male peacock spreads his beautiful tail feathers in a display to attract a mate.

Below: Bats use sound waves to locate food and to navigate. Their high pitched squeaks bounce off any objects in their path and the bats can detect the echo.

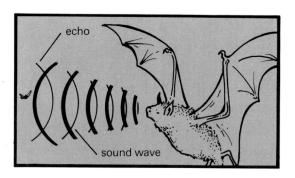

echo

sound wave

Animals communicate with each other by sounds and gestures just as humans do. They also use their sense of touch and smell — senses which are not so well developed in humans. Animals communicate with each other to find a mate, to warn of danger, to tell where food is to be found or to mark the ownership of a territory.

Birds sing during the breeding season to claim territory and to attract a mate. The blackbird has a loud alarm call to warn other blackbirds when danger threatens. Wolves have a special howl which gathers the whole pack together. And a mother seal can locate her pup on a crowded beach by recognizing

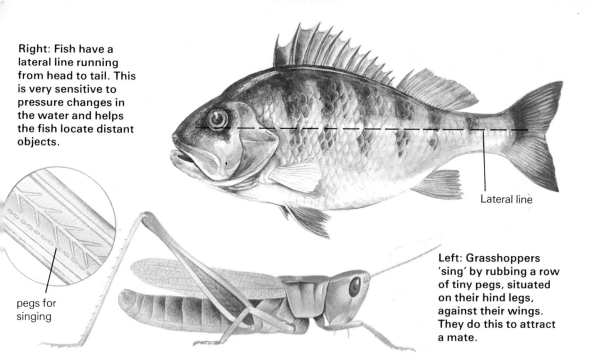

Right: Fish have a lateral line running from head to tail. This is very sensitive to pressure changes in the water and helps the fish locate distant objects.

Lateral line

pegs for singing

Left: Grasshoppers 'sing' by rubbing a row of tiny pegs, situated on their hind legs, against their wings. They do this to attract a mate.

Below: Great crested grebes 'dance' together during the breeding season. They offer each other weeds.

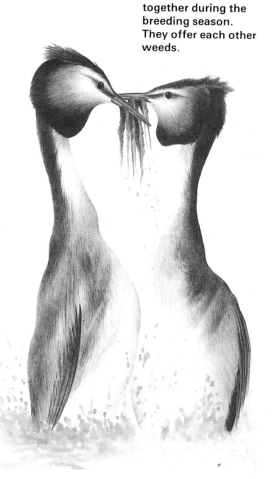

its cry. Whales and dolphins use a great range of noises to communicate with each other underwater.

Special gestures and actions are used by many animals during the breeding season. Some birds spread their brightly coloured feathers or perform special movements or 'dances' to attract a mate. Animals also have special gestures to warn each other of danger or to threaten attack. Rabbits thump their hind legs on the ground to signal danger. A chimpanzee opens its eyes wide and closes its lips to show aggression.

Smell

Animals have a very strong sense of smell. The special scents or 'pheromones' they produce are one of the main ways that many communicate with each other. Dogs mark their territory with their scent. Some fish use scent to signal danger, while other animals attract a mate or recognize their young by it. Some people say that honey bees produce special scents to tell each other where a food source is. Certain male moths such as the emperor moth can sense the pheromones of a female from a couple of kilometres away.

25

Animal Journeys

Many animals make long journeys in search of food and to their breeding grounds. Herbivores such as elephants that live in herds, spend much of their lives wandering in search of food. Some like the caribou of North America make regular journeys or migrations each year. The caribou breeds in

Above: The monarch butterfly of North America flies thousands of kilometres when it migrates for the winter. It often travels as far south as Mexico.

Left: The Arctic tern spends summer in the Arctic then flies some 19,000 km south to Antarctica for the summer.

Right: Eels breed in the Sargasso Sea. The youngsters then swim to the rivers of North America and Europe where they spend their adult lives (see map below). They return to the Sargasso Sea to lay their eggs and die.

the Arctic tundra during the summer and then travels to forests further south for the winter. Large herds of wildebeest in East Africa travel from one end of the Serengetti to the other and back again each year, as they follow the rains for the best grazing.

Many sea mammals and fish swim great distances. The grey whale travels some 20,000 kilometres on annual migrations between its feeding grounds in the Arctic and its breeding grounds further south. The green turtle swims hundreds of kilometres to lay its eggs on the beach where it was born. Salmon travel from the oceans to freshwater streams to mate and lay their eggs. Each salmon uses its sense of smell to find its way to the particular river or stream where it was born. The young salmon swim down to the sea when they are about one year old. They stay there until they are mature enough to breed.

Many insects, particularly moths and butterflies, also travel long distances on their seasonal migrations, and a few even cross seas. Each summer some painted lady and clouded yellow butterflies cross the Channel from the continent to England.

Bird Migrations

Some of the longest journeys are made by birds when they migrate to and from warmer climates. Many, such as the swallow and house martin, breed during the summer months in Europe, then gather in large flocks to fly to Africa as soon as winter approaches and their food supply of insects dies out. They choose the shortest sea crossings, feeding frequently along the way.

Snow geese and blue geese make the longest non-stop flights. They fly over 2400 kilometres from Hudson Bay in Canada to the Gulf of Mexico. Some seabirds make particularly long journeys. The Arctic tern, for example, travels from the Arctic to the Antarctic so that it can spend summer at both places.

We do not completely understand how birds manage to find their way when they migrate. Experiments have shown that many birds navigate by the Earth's magnetism and the direction of the Sun. Birds know when it is time to set off by the changes in the length of daylight hours, rather than by changes in temperature.

Herds of musk oxen travel from river valleys and lake shores to spend the winter on high ground. The freezing Arctic gales in these exposed places prevent snow from burying the lichens and berries that they feed on.

Animal Defences

Animals have evolved many wonderful methods of defending themselves against their attackers. Some, such as the antelope and cattle, have horns for weapons; others have armour, like the tortoise and the pangolin. Some simply run swiftly from their hunters. The zebra and gazelle are both very fast runners. Many of the smaller creatures use a poisonous sting to protect themselves. Spiders and wasps do this.

Some animals use camouflage as defence. This means they blend into their background and cannot easily be seen. The chameleon can change its colour very rapidly and with great variety — it can become green, yellow, cream or dark brown, and can even make its spots lighter or darker.

Birds and insects also use camouflage, their colours merging with the colour of their surroundings. Even a large animal like the zebra can stand against the bushes on the African savannah and not be noticed.

Another form of defence is mimicry. Some animals are disguised as creatures or plants which are not eaten by would-be enemies. For example, hoverflies look like wasps. Their enemies will not eat them for fear of being stung. Some moths look just like dead leaves; there is even one that looks like a bird-dropping when it folds its wings. Another example of this form of defence is the way the stick insect lies so still and appears to be part of a twig.

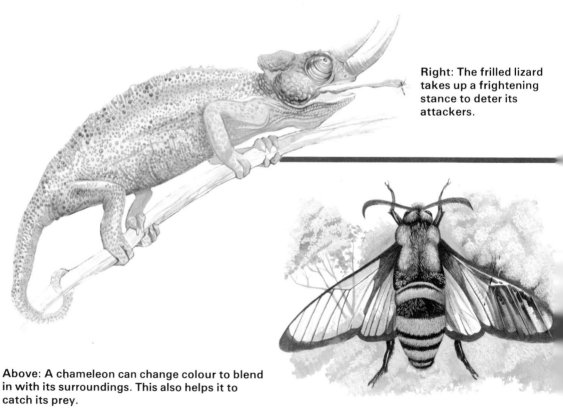

Right: The frilled lizard takes up a frightening stance to deter its attackers.

Above: A chameleon can change colour to blend in with its surroundings. This also helps it to catch its prey.

Above: Some moths mimic or copy other insects such as wasps and bees, and so gain protection from their enemies.

Some animals bluff their enemies by pretending to be much more fearsome than they really are. The Australian frilled lizard is a harmless creature, but when attacked it spreads out a fold of skin to form a ruff around its neck and hisses very loudly to frighten its attacker. The North American opossum, on the other hand, makes no attempt to be aggressive. It lies still and pretends to be dead — it 'plays possum'!

The skunk uses a very unpleasant form of defence. It has two special glands near its tail, and if threatened will shoot a vile smelling liquid at its attacker. It can shoot it over three metres with good aim.

Many animals are protected by either a kind of armour plating or spines over their bodies. The tortoise, for instance, can completely withdraw its head and legs inside its shell which cannot be penetrated. The pangolin, or scaly anteater, is covered with horny overlapping scales. It can roll up into a tight ball for safety. The hedgehog, which is covered in prickles, also uses this defence and rolls into a small tight ball. But the porcupine which has strong stiff quills all over its body, simply lashes out at an attacker with its quilled tail. The quills stick fast in the attacker's body, often causing fatal wounds.

Right: Pangolins roll up into a tight ball, protected by their scaly armour plating.

Large animals such as the elephant need no defensive weapons. Their size is defence enough — a charging elephant or rhinoceros would intimidate any would-be hunter. But musk-oxen, which live in the Arctic regions, have short legs and cannot run away fast from a pack of wolves. So they form a tight circle, facing outwards, with their young safely protected in their midst. Deer, bison and other hoofed mammals live in herds as a means of protection.

So, although many creatures seem to exist as a tasty meal, nature has provided them with a wonderful variety of defences.

Above: The North American possum plays dead in order to deceive its enemies. Most animals prefer live prey.

Life in Water

The earliest forms of life are believed to have lived in the oceans which, at that time, covered nearly the whole planet. Today the oceans still cover more than two-thirds of Earth's surface and contain a vast range of life.

Some animals are so small that they cannot be seen with the naked eye. These are the minute creatures that, along with

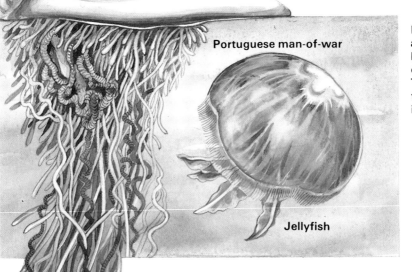

Portuguese man-of-war

Jellyfish

Right: The blue shark and all its relatives have skeletons made of cartilage not bone. This shark is one of the fiercest predators in the sea.

Above: The Portuguese man-of-war is a coelenterate, which means 'hollow bodied'. It looks like a jellyfish but is in fact a colony of tiny animals, called hydrozoans, which hang in long strings from a gas filled float. Its 'tentacles' often grow as long as 18 metres. Jellyfish move by a kind of jet propulsion or drift on the sea currents. Some have stings which can cause great pain to humans.

simple plants, form the plankton which floats at, or near, the water's surface. The largest animal on Earth, the blue whale, feeds on the small crustaceans that form part of the plankton. Whales are mammals and, although they live in the sea, they need to surface frequently to breath. Fish, however, can breath in water because they have gills.

Many fish, such as the herring and mackerel, protect themselves from enemies by living in large shoals. Others, like the rays and certain sharks, prefer to lead solitary lives.

Most fish swim by moving their bodies from side to side, and use their fins for steering and braking. Other creatures have different methods of moving. Jellyfish often keep quite still and let the ocean currents carry them along, while squids use a form of jet propulsion.

Left: The shrimp is a crustacean — an animal with a flexible jointed shell or crust. Some live deep in the ocean and others live in fresh waters.

Below: Mudskippers live in mangrove swamps and spend as much time out of the water as in it. They use their fins to pull themselves along on land.

Mouth open

Gill cover closed

Mouth closed

Gill cover open

Life on the Ocean Floor

Deep in the oceans, it is dark. No plants can survive so many animals depend on debris floating down from above. Tiny scavenging worms, sea cucumbers and small crustaceans live there as well as some strange fish. Many are blind, and others like the viperfish, have luminous spots on their bodies which help them find their way or attract prey or a mate. Some have huge mouths to catch falling particles or to eat fish the same size as themselves.

Right: Fish breathe with special organs called gills. Through its mouth, a fish draws in water which then flows over the gills. Oxygen in the water passes into the blood supply of the gill tissue and waste carbon dioxide is washed away into the water.

On the Seashore

Sandy beaches and rocky shores provide a home for a great number of animals and plants. Some live in sand dunes above the shore; some beneath the sand itself, some cling to rocks, while others live in rock pools.

Sand dunes provide a home for spiders, digger wasps and grasshoppers. Rabbits will often live among sand hills covered in marram grass, and sometimes owls hunt

feathery antennae to strain food particles from the water. When the tide goes out most burrowing animals stay buried and wait for the sea to return.

Small animals of the shore provide food for many species of wading bird. Some, like the redshank, have long bills that probe into the sand, while others, like the oyster-catcher, can prise open cockles and other seashells.

Right: Rock pools provide a home for a great variety of plant and animal life. Seaweeds and other algae grow on the rocks. Limpets and periwinkles feed on the algae. Sea anemones attach themselves to the rocks and crabs and starfish shelter beneath them. Razorshells, gapers and various worms live buried in sand.

1) Limpet; 2) Sea anemone;
3) Periwinkle; 4) Slipper limpet shell;
5) Whelk; 6) Thin tellin; 7) Razorshell;
8) Sand gaper; 9) Parchment worm.

there in the winter. At the top of a beach the sand is only wetted by sea-spray or by very high tides. Gulls, flies and sand-hoppers feed there on seaweed washed up by the sea.

Beneath the Sand

Beneath the sand which is regularly covered by tides live burrowing animals such as the lugworm, the clam, the sea-mouse and the ghost shrimp. All these creatures feed when the tide is in.

Some take in seawater and food particles by sucking through a tube. Others use their

Rock pools

Rock pools appear at low tide and the animals that live on the rocks are left without water. Such creatures include the mussel and barnacle which, at low-tide, seal their shells tightly shut keeping some seawater inside to stay moist. Seaweed and other algae are plants. Some grow on the rocks and provide homes and hiding places for the many animals that live in the rock pools. Crabs, several kinds of shrimps, small fish, dog welks and periwinkles are all found in rock pools.

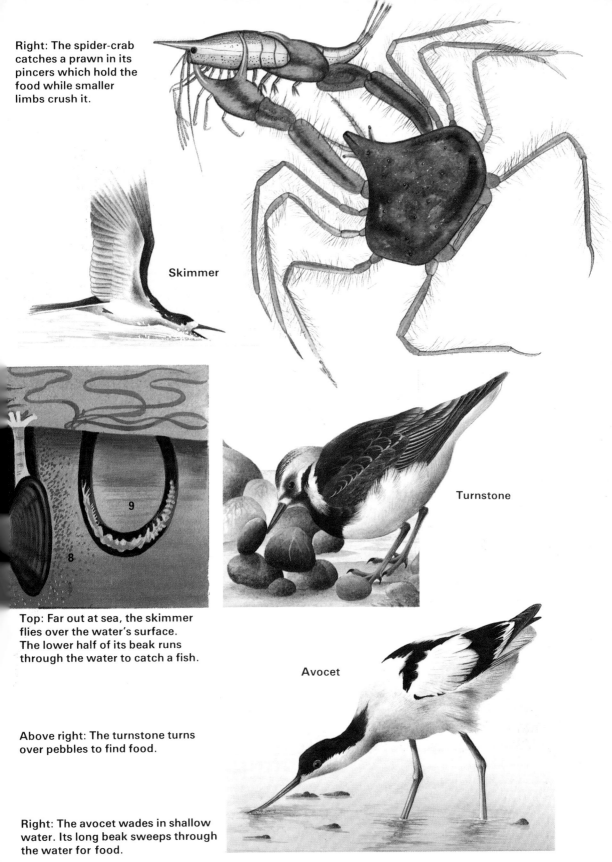

Right: The spider-crab catches a prawn in its pincers which hold the food while smaller limbs crush it.

Skimmer

Turnstone

Avocet

Top: Far out at sea, the skimmer flies over the water's surface. The lower half of its beak runs through the water to catch a fish.

Above right: The turnstone turns over pebbles to find food.

Right: The avocet wades in shallow water. Its long beak sweeps through the water for food.

The World of Birds

Birds can be found in nearly every part of the world. They have even been seen near the icy North and South Poles, and flying close to the summits of high mountains.

There are over 8,000 different kinds of birds living in the world. Many species have difficulty in surviving because their habitats are being destroyed by man, or because they are hunted for food or for their feathers. Some kinds of birds, such as the passenger pigeon, the great auk and the dodo, are now extinct because of man's activities. Other birds, such as the sparrow and starling, have lived successfully alongside man and spread throughout the world.

The dodo, a flightless bird that lived on Mauritius, is now extinct.

Left: Pheasants do not fly well and live mainly on the ground. They roam the fields in winter looking for food.

Above: The razorbill has webbed feet and is an excellent swimmer, but cannot walk well on land. It nests in colonies on sea cliffs and feeds on fish which it dives for in the sea.

Above: Waxwings have feet that are suited to perching on twigs and beaks adapted to eating berries.

Above: The eagle is a bird of prey. It has sharp curved claws, or talons, for catching its prey and a hooked beak for tearing flesh.

Birds feed on a great variety of foods. The size of a bird, and the shape of its beak and claws are suited to the type of food it eats. Seed- and nut-eating species, such as the finches, are small and light so that they can perch on light twigs to reach their food. Woodpeckers and nuthatches have pointed beaks to probe bark for insects. Ducks have bills with toothed edges for filtering food from water and, like most other waterbirds, webbed feet for swimming. Birds of prey hunt small animals. Their sharp talons catch and kill the prey and their hooked beaks tear the food into pieces.

Not all birds leave the ground to find food or to nest. Game birds, such as the pheasant, do not fly easily and only take to the air when forced to. In contrast, many seabirds spend most of their lives flying. Frigate-birds can glide over the water for hours, occasionally diving down to snatch a fish from the surface.

The smallest bird is the bee humming-bird. It is only 5.7cm long. Humming-birds can beat their wings so fast that they almost become invisible. They hover motionless in front of flowers and feed on the nectar.

Bee humming-bird

The largest bird is the ostrich. It is too heavy to fly but can run extremely fast when threatened by enemies. Ostriches, which can grow up to 2.5 metres tall, live on the grasslands of Africa.

35

Birds in Flight

The flightless cassowary lives in dense forests in Australia and New Guinea, where it has few enemies apart from man. Its legs are very strong and its feet have strong toes.

Emus, kiwis and ostriches live permanently on the ground. They have strong legs and can run fast but they cannot use their wings to fly. The penguin cannot fly either; its wings are used for swimming instead.

Most other species of birds can fly and their bodies are well adapted to life in the air. The skeleton of a bird is very light. Many of the large bones are hollow and the smaller bones are thin and delicate. Powerful muscles, attached to the bird's breastbone, move the wings.

Small feathers called coverts cover a bird's body and give the wings a smooth surface, while larger primary and secondary feathers help to keep the bird aloft. Birds spend quite a lot of time cleaning, or preening, their feathers. Most birds also spread oil, from a special gland above the tail, over their feathers to keep them in good condition.

Birds usually fly by flapping their wings up and down. Fast-flying birds, such as the swift, have narrow wings while crows and other slow-flying birds have broader ones.

Above: As a bird beats its wings down, the feathers close to force air down and backwards.

Right: Swallows have long, narrow wings and are fast agile fliers but they do not walk well on land. They eat insects which they catch in flight. Each year they fly hundreds of kilometres to spend winter in Africa, returning to Europe in the spring to breed.

Above: Penguins have flipper-like wings to swim through water. They cannot fly.

Left: Swifts are very fast flying birds and hardly ever land on the ground.

Feathers are made of keratin, the substance our nails and hair are made of. Fluffy down feathers lie close to the body and keep the bird warm. Stiff covert feathers cover the body and wings. The flight feathers on the wings are the longest.

Above: As a bird moves its wings upwards, the feathers part to allow air through so that the bird does not lose height.

Birds such as the condor have long broad wings and can soar through the air, riding air currents with great skill. Soaring in this way uses little energy because the bird does not have to beat its wings.

When a bird wants to take off it leaps into the air and beats its wings as fast as it can. Some waterbirds, such as the swan, cannot leap into the air and have to run along the water's surface flapping their wings before they take off. When birds want to land they slow down by spreading their wings and tail like a parachute.

The World of Insects

Insects are the most numerous of all living creatures. They represent about 80 per cent of all animal species. There are more than one million known insect species on Earth and probably just as many still undiscovered. They live in just about every kind of habitat from the Arctic and Antartic to the Equator. Some survive beneath snow and ice, or in deserts, while others can live in salt lakes or hot springs.

What is an insect

All insects have bodies that are divided into three main parts: the head, the thorax and the abdomen. On their heads they have a pair of antennae, used mainly for feeding and smelling. Insects have three pairs of jointed legs which enable them to move quickly and easily.

Apart from birds and bats, insects are the only other kind of animals that can fly properly. Most insects have one or two pairs of wings attached to the thorax, the middle section of their body. Beetles have a hard wing case which covers a second pair of wings used for flying. Some types of insects have no wings and, instead of flying, may be able to run or jump long distances. Silverfish, for example, are non-flying insects and can be seen at night inside houses. A flea has no wings but can jump distances a hundred times its own length. This is how it moves from one animal host to another.

Many insects live alone except during the breeding season. Others, such as bees and ants, live in highly organized colonies sharing food and work. They are called social insects (see page 22).

Insects feed on plants and animals. Some, such as the cockroach, will eat almost anything, but most feed on one particular

Spider

Fly

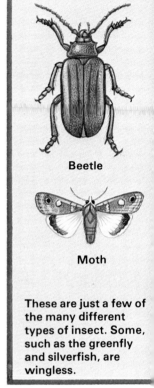

Beetle

Moth

Above: A spider is not an insect. It has eight legs and only two main parts to its body. An insect has six legs, three parts to its body and usually one or two pairs of wings.

These are just a few of the many different types of insect. Some, such as the greenfly and silverfish, are wingless.

Bees are social insects and live together in a colony. The worker bees provide food and care for the young once mating is over.

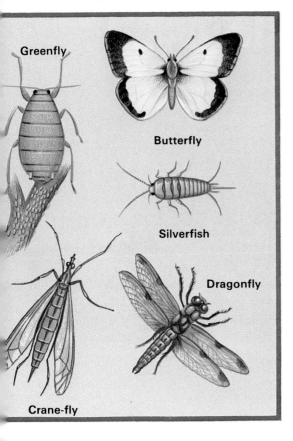

Greenfly

Butterfly

Silverfish

Dragonfly

Crane-fly

The antlion is the larva of a flying insect. It eats ants, which it catches by digging a pit and lying in wait until a passing ant falls in.

kind of food. The larvae and nymphs may feed on different things from the adult insect. The carnivores have many different ways of catching prey. Dragonflies are swift flyers and overpower other insects in flight. Antlions dig holes to trap ants, and wasps sting caterpillars to death.

Insect Life Stories

Insects undergo a process called metamorphosis (see page 21). Some, such as butterflies, hatch from eggs and grow as wingless larvae until they pupate. The transformation into the adult form takes place inside the pupa. Other insects, such as the dragonfly, do not pupate. Instead the insect hatches from the egg in a wingless form called a nymph. The nymph moults many times as it grows, emerging from the final moult as a winged adult.

Insects and man

Many plant-eating insects are considered pests because they destroy our crops and garden plants. The aphid, or greenfly, damages plants by sucking out sap. The ladybird is liked by gardeners because it eats aphids. Locusts can destroy vast quantities of food crops, descending in swarms that can number millions of insects. Other insects are of great use to man. Bees are used to pollinate certain crops and also produce honey and wax.

Below: Sometimes millions of locusts gather together in a swarm. They can destroy whole fields full of crops very quickly and used to cause local communities to starve.

39

Animal Records

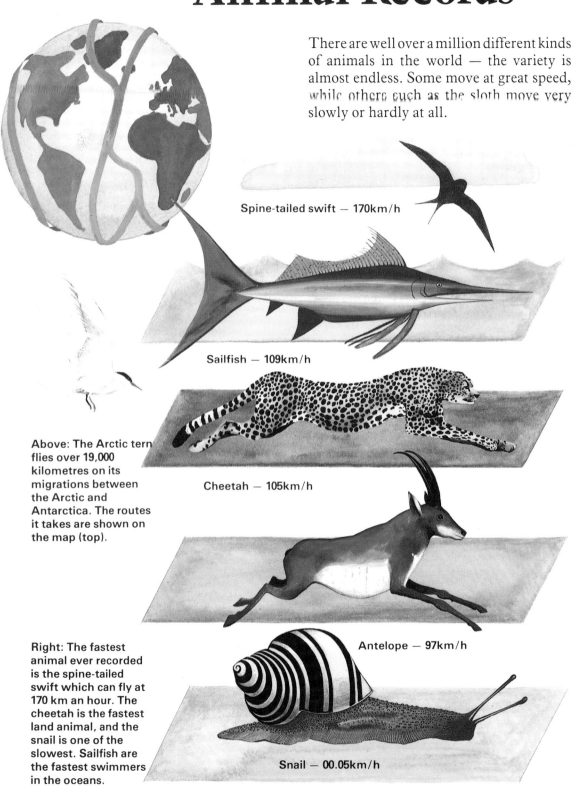

There are well over a million different kinds of animals in the world — the variety is almost endless. Some move at great speed, while others such as the sloth move very slowly or hardly at all.

Spine-tailed swift — 170km/h

Sailfish — 109km/h

Above: The Arctic tern flies over 19,000 kilometres on its migrations between the Arctic and Antarctica. The routes it takes are shown on the map (top).

Cheetah — 105km/h

Antelope — 97km/h

Right: The fastest animal ever recorded is the spine-tailed swift which can fly at 170 km an hour. The cheetah is the fastest land animal, and the snail is one of the slowest. Sailfish are the fastest swimmers in the oceans.

Snail — 00.05km/h

Animals vary tremendously in size and weight. The male African elephant can reach a height of over three metres and weigh more than eight tonnes. In contrast, the pygmy shrew is only 5.7cm long and weighs less than 3g. The wandering albatross has the longest wings. It measures more than three metres from wing tip to wing tip.

Tortoise

Compared to most animals, human beings have long lives but they do not live as long as some tortoises. The oldest tortoise ever recorded was 152 years old.

The oldest known bird was an Andean condor that lived for 72 years in a zoo in Russia.

Below: The largest living animal is the blue whale. It can grow to 30 metres in length and weigh more than 150 tonnes. The elephant is the largest land animal and the giraffe the tallest.

Wonders of the Plant World

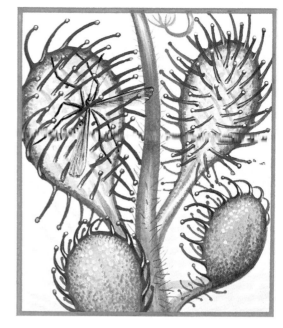

Plants can be found in nearly every region of the world. One group of plants, called lichens, have even been found growing within 400 kilometres of the South Pole and on rocks too hot to touch. A lichen is made up of two plants, a fungus and an alga, which live closely together and help each other. If temperatures are too extreme, the lichens dry out but they can often start to grow again when conditions improve.

Most plants contain a green pigment called chlorophyll which, using sunlight for energy, allows them to make their own food. Fungi contain no chlorophyll and have to feed off other plants and animals, living and dead. The mushrooms we eat and the moulds that grow on stale bread are all types of fungi.

As well as water and sunlight, plants need nutrients to grow well. Some plants, such as sundews, that grow in places where there are few nutrients, get extra nourishment by trapping and digesting insects. The Venus fly-trap has hinged leaves. When an insect steps on the hairs which line the leaves, the leaves close trapping the insect. Pitcher plants grow on trees, catching the water they need in their vase-shaped leaves.

Below: Bromeliads are epiphytes or air plants. They grow on the branches or trunks of trees.

Above: Sundews are insectivorous plants. They trap insects on their glue-tipped hairs.

Below: Rafflesia grows on lianas in the tropical forests of South East Asia. It has neither stem nor leaves and feeds off its host. Its flower is the largest in the world.

Above: The longest lived plant is the bristle-cone pine. Some trees are more than 4600 years old.

Right: The largest living plant is a giant sequoia. It is 84 metres tall and 9.6 metres in diameter.

Insects drown in the 'vase' and provide the plants with nutrients.

Mistletoe is a parasite. It takes water from the tree it grows on. Certain parasites take food as well as water from their host and often do great harm. Some plants grow on other plants to get closer to sunlight. These are known as epiphytes or air plants, and include many ferns, mosses, lichens and orchids. They make their own food and do not harm the tree they grow on.

Algae are the smallest plants. Many are microscopic and millions can exist unseen in a litre of seawater. The largest plants are certain trees belonging to the conifer family. The tallest tree in the world today is a Californian redwood which is 112 metres high. The most massive living tree, with the broadest trunk, is a giant sequoia in California. It is called the General Sherman tree. The longest living plants are bristle-cone pines that grow on high mountains in north-western America.

Index

THE WONDERS OF NATURE
LIFE BEFORE MAN
THE CHALLENGE OF SPACE
THE WORLD OF SPEED